Through The Heart's Eyes

Through The Heart's Eyes

Love Poems by Alexandra Vasiliu
Illustrated by Andreea Dumez

Stairway Books

Boston

Through The Heart's Eyes: Love Poems by Alexandra Vasiliu. Illustrated by Andreea Dumez. Boston. Stairway Books, 2021

ISBN-13: 978-0997008937

To all those who see their loved one
through the heart's eyes

CONTENTS

Through The Heart's Eyes

The Most Wanted Trip

If you're planning a getaway
to the end of the world,
take me with you.
Love will make us run fast,
so fast we will feel
as though we're barely touching
the ground.
Our hearts will soar high,
wander amid billions of stars,
catch rainbows,
and roam freely
to every corner of this world.
Take me with you
wherever you want to go.
Our love will be the best journey
of our lifetime.

Our Happiness

Last night,
I told you,
"Let's settle somewhere
at the end of the world,
where winters are
but a distant memory
and happiness is found all around us."

"Where is the end of the world?"
you asked me with a laugh.

"Anywhere we want.
It could be just around the corner,
or somewhere remote
where we can watch
the most beautiful sunsets
in the world
and catch shooting stars
in our hands."

You closed your eyes
and kissed me.
In a heartbeat,
we discovered that magical place.

Thank you, my love,
for showing me
that happiness
can flourish
on every inch
of this earth.

Watching From Afar

With you by my side,
I feel lighthearted
as though I live on the moon
floating over all worldly things.

Like spectators,
we watch everything from afar.
There is so much taking place
all around us:
many crises,
uprisings and conflicts,
and so much suffering.

You put your arm
around my shoulders
and I quickly find my way back
home.

With you by my side,
I close my eyes
and make a wish.
"May we always look
within ourselves
through the eyes of our hearts.
May we always find our love
growing,
glowing,
and reigning in our hearts.
May we always belong
to the essence of all things—
love."

Happy

In the City of Lights,
while we were walking
hand in hand,
I wanted to stop the earth
from spinning
and halt the passage of time.

"There is so much beauty in love.
I wish
the constant rat race of life would stop
so everybody could notice that."

You smiled and said,
"How boldly beautiful of you.
Even in this luxurious city,
you think of love
and noble things.

This is why
I love you so much.
May you always stay
an unselfish,
hopeful romantic.
May happiness never find a reason
to leave our sides."

The Peace Of Your Love

As the rivers return
to the arms of the seas,
so too does my soul
search for you,
looking and yearning
for the peace of your love.

Run Away With Me

Run away with me
to a faraway place
where the sun of love rises
to greet us every morning,
yet not a beautiful thought dies.

Run away with me
to a faraway place
where the moon of passion glows for us
every night,
yet not a dream falls asleep.

Run away with me
to a faraway place
where the stars dance in our palms,
yet not a loving word is lost.

Run away with me
to a faraway place
where we will always have room
to grow and thrive,
yet time will never leave wrinkles upon our hearts.

Over The Bridge Of Words

"Let's cross the bridge of words,"
you once told me.
"We will never need so many words
to understand each other.
Take my hand, my love.
One day,
we will arrive
on the other side of the bridge
where we will speak in feelings."

I held your hand
and ran with you
as fast as I could.
I dreamed of speaking in love
with you
in no time.

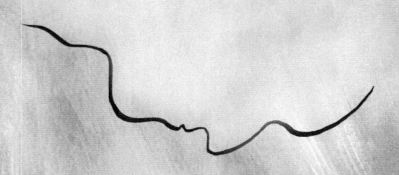

With My Closed Eyes

Whenever I think of you,
I close my eyes
and see you
deep down in my heart.
I admire you, my love,
in all your splendor,
as illuminated
and naked
as only a beautiful soul can be.

At Home

You always help me
feel at home
in the blink of an eye.

You capture my lips
with a kiss
and sweep me up
with your love
all the way back
into your heart.

Isn't this magical?

Many Eyes

This is my secret:
my heart can see you
everywhere,
using the eyes
of thirst,
of hunger,
of yearning,
of love,
and of passion.

Mail From An Angel

One winter morning,
in front of my door,
I found a couple of footprints
in the freshly fallen snow.

"Where did they come from?
And where do they lead?"
I asked myself.
"Have I received mail
from an angel?"

I looked closer
and saw two words
wreathed with roses:
"Protect love."

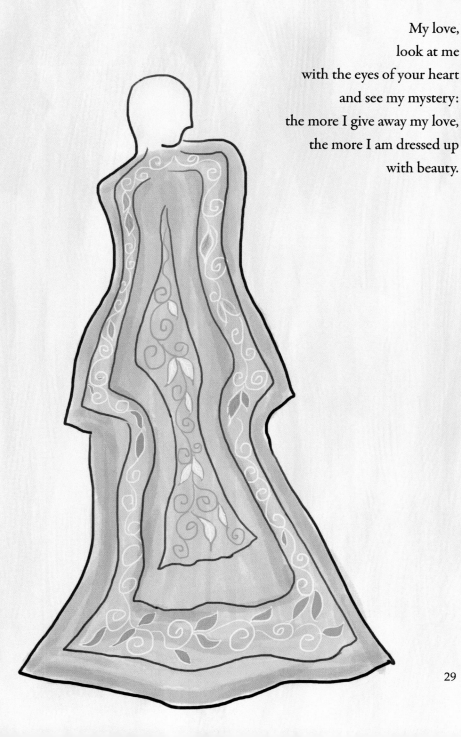

Dressed Up With Beauty

My love,
look at me
with the eyes of your heart
and see my mystery:
the more I give away my love,
the more I am dressed up
with beauty.

To Belong To You

Since we first met,
my heart has been restless.
I only wanted
to belong to you.
I continually prayed for us, wishing,
"May love engulf us with joy.
May love make us wonder,
Where is the earth?
Where is everybody else?
May love be an endless bliss for us."

Of All The Impossible Things

My love,
of all the impossible things
I crave to do
on this earth,
I only want to embrace you
like the night hugs the moon,
and give you
all the little stars of my heart.

Waiting

I have waited for you
for a thousand years.
And when you came into my life,
the eternity of love began.

Our Dream

There was something mysterious
that dwelled in our hearts,
something magnetic
that kept drawing us in
and made us run
over rainbows, stars, and planets.

"Don't be afraid, my dear,"
you said.

"Close your eyes
and see with your heart.

34

"What drives us
is not an earthly desire.
It is a celestial dream of love.
It is a fabulous path
waiting for us
at the beginning
of the world.
We are called to bring
this heavenly dream to life.
This will be
the crowning achievement
of our love."

Our Secret Palace

Come faster to me
on the wings of hope,
and leave all worldly troubles
behind you.
Let's build a shelter
in our secret palace of love.

Throw away the key
when you arrive.
The storms of life will not hit us.
Come faster to me,
to a place created just for us,
where we will feel whole together.

One

Since I fell in love with you,
I have kept a secret hope
in my heart.

Day after day,
night after night,
I have prayed for us
to become one
like two united rays of light.

I have prayed so fervently for us,
my heart striving fiercely
until I wove a luminous dress
with all my thoughts and feelings.
"I will wear this dress
for the rest of my life,"
I said to myself.
"This beautiful dress is a reminder
that anything can be given to you
when you ask
with a pure heart."

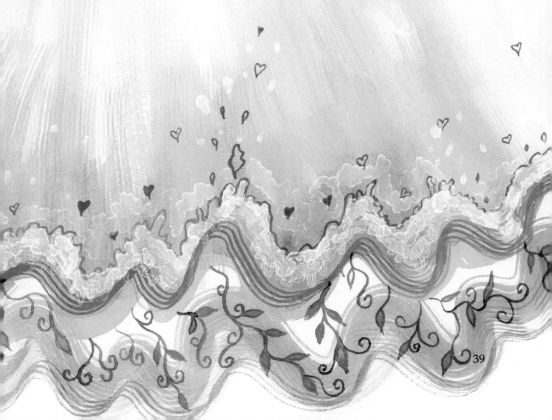

Your Love Poem

Your fire burns my body;
your whispers call me closer
to feel the heat of your heart.
I am the embodiment
of a love dream,
brought to life
and sculpted by your hands.
You touch my body
as you would shape clay,
changing me into a rose
in full bloom,
a dove flying free,
and a soft melody
that you love fully
without knowing
all the lyrics.
I am a woman of flames
and pieces of sky.
I am an amalgam
of dreams and unique poems.
I am a mosaic of wishes and desires.
Through your touch,
I become love.
Through your touch,
I become a poem.
Your beautiful love poem.

Let's Catch Happiness

You once told me,
"Happiness has long legs.
It runs fast."

"Don't worry, my love,"
I answered you.
"We will keep pace.
We must run as swiftly
as athletes competing
for first place.
All obstacles in our path
will be but a blur

as we pass them by
and let nothing stand in our way.
We will have no worries other than
to run faster and faster,
so that we can catch happiness
in our hearts."

Words Of Love

Last night,
I had a dream.

It seemed
I locked up an abundance
of love words
deep in my soul.

I woke up trembling
and rushed to release them.

I whispered to the words
hidden deep in my chest,
"May you all fly with haste
to my beloved
and build a nest of love
in his heart.
Empower him with the ability
to trust in my love.
Make his heart thrive with joy.
Fly to my beloved now
and deliver
all my incandescent feelings
for him."

Silence

In a moment of silence,
I heard your footsteps
entering my heart.
When I opened the door,
a sweep of swallows
stormed inside.
But as I looked closer,
I saw they were your kisses
landing
on the nest of my feelings.

Thinking Of You

I was thinking of you
for so long
that my heart grew wings
and turned into a bird
flying tirelessly around you,
always looking for your smile.

Yours

I want to be beautiful
only for you.
Beautiful like the sea
kissing the horizon.

Beautiful like the night
in the moon's arms.

Beautiful like the fresh snow
blanketing the ground.
Beautiful like the stars
reflecting in tranquil waters.

I want to be beautiful.
Beautiful only for you.

Another Apple

When you touched my heart,
you said,
"I feel like I have been
to paradise
and bitten a new apple."

"Maybe,"
I said,
"but my love,
you did not discover
the tree bearing the knowledge
of good and evil.
Yet you definitely tasted
the unforgettable sweetness
of my love."

Like In A Small Frame

I came close to my beloved
and saw a window
in his chest.

Bending,
I looked inside.

Both of us were there
kissing within his heart.

The Flower Of Hope

When we first met,
I fell in love with you easily.

The walls of my heart crumbled,
making room
for a gorgeous flower of hope
to blossom.

In that moment
I promised myself,

"From now on,
I will nurture this sweet flower
inside my heart,
with all my love and grace."

I know
that one day,
you will notice my treasure
with the eyes
of your heart.
On that day,
you will see me—
my soul,
my essence.

And you will ask yourself,
"How can she carry
so much beauty deep inside her?
Her mystery is captivating,
her grace is boundless,
her flower is irreplaceable,
her femininity is incredible.
I can't live without this woman."

I hope
from that day on
you will love me even more.

Now I Know

The more I love you,
the more I realize
how much more I can still love you.
I think of you constantly,
and wish
all the best for you.

May your heart always be
full of happiness and peace.
May your soul always find
serenity and bliss.

There is no end to my love for you.

The To-Do List Of A Lifetime

love

dream

believe in miracles

caress

hug

kiss

give

cherish

grow

bloom

protect

forget
forgive
heal
rise
love again
search for happiness
make peace
spread light
hope
love more
and even more

Dancing

Last night,
we danced
on moonbeams
and flitted around the earth
like two untamed souls.

We danced
until the sky parted
and sprinkled confetti
around us.

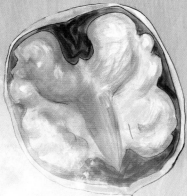

We danced
until the world shrank
to the size of a tiny walnut
and we couldn't see it anymore.

We danced
and played like children,
feeling reborn,
in a state of pure bliss.
We danced
until we shimmered
like a new galaxy.

We were born
to shine together.
We were born
to bloom together.

Two Suns

I wanted
to gaze into your eyes.
But I couldn't see them
anymore.

Instead,
you had two suns
radiating your love
for me.

All The Sweet Names

My love,
you might count
every grain of sand
on all the beaches
in the world,
yet you will never have
enough time to learn
all the sweet names
my heart has given you.
You will never know
how deeply and beautifully
you have rooted
in my soul.
You are my whole universe.

My Love Is A River

My love is a river
continuouisly flowing with
streams of hope,
joy
and light.
Come close to me,
dive into my waters,
and quench
the thirst of your heart.
I will give
all my love
to you unconditionally.

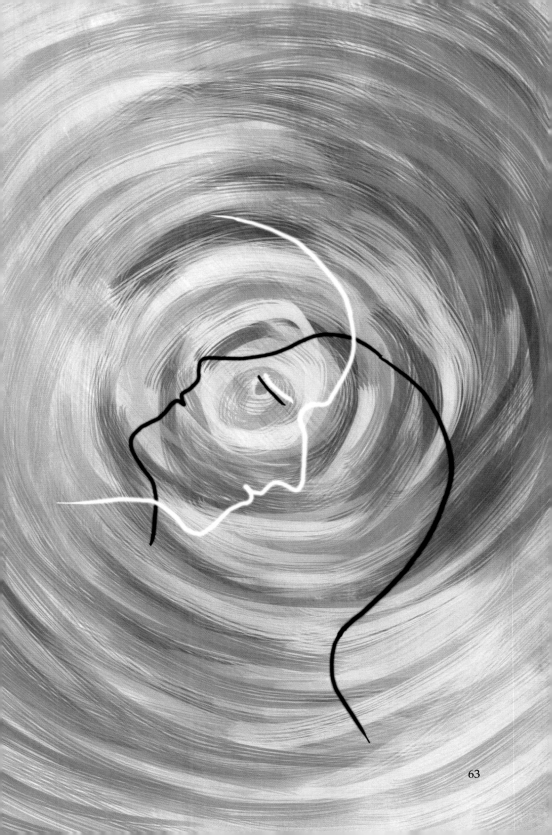

63

Cosmic Flowers

Last night,
you lifted your hand
in the air
and plucked hundreds of stars
from the sky.

"Darling,
I have just picked
cosmic flowers
for you.
Let me place them
in your hair,"
you said.
"I want you to smell
like spring
tonight."

Our House

Build a house for us,
where the forests of hope
grow all around us,
where the twinkling stars of love
bloom in abundance
like perennial flowers,
where the oceans of longing
hold the memory of joy.
Build a place for us
and take me with you.
I want to leave behind
all the environs of uncertainty.
I want to be with you
and live
in our house of love
forever.
Build a house for us
and welcome me
like I would enter paradise.

See Everything Differently

My darling,
let's protect
the words of love
so they never become
endangered species.

Let's save them
from going extinct.

Let's give them
a new life
in our hearts,
so they can be nurtured
and grow within us.

Let's make them bloom

every day
on our lips.

All I want is
to speak in love
and kindness
with you.

Dear Reader,

Thank you very much for reading my book.

I hope that my poems helped you see your soulmate with the eyes of your heart. If so, please take a moment and show your appreciation by writing a short review on the website where you purchased this book. Your support means a lot to me. Thank you very much, beautiful soul.

With love and poetry,
Alexandra

About The Author

Alexandra Vasiliu is an award-winning poet and a believer in the power of seeing with your heart's eyes. She has been composing poems for as long as she can remember.

She has a PhD in Medieval Literature, and is the author of the inspirational poetry collections *Blooming*, *Healing Words*, and *Be My Moon*.

When she isn't busy writing, she loves reading uplifting poems, gazing inward at her heart, and admiring her soulmate.

Read more about Alexandra by visiting her website and her social media pages:

www.alexandravasiliu.net
www.instagram.com/alexandravasiliuwriter/
www.pinterest.com/AlVasiliuWriter/

About The Illustrator

Andreea has been painting and drawing from a young age, and her earliest memories relate to having a pencil in her hand. Sometimes her dancing fairies and heroes would go wandering, later turning up on the walls of her house or on the pages of her parents' planners.

After graduating from the Fine Arts University and the Pharmacy Faculty in Bucharest, she continued her lifelong dream in the domain of the creative arts. Her illustrations evoke her childhood imagination and her experience as a professional artist.

She is currently living and working in New Hampshire, USA, participating in art exhibits both locally and in Boston.

You can find out more about her artwork on:

www.andreeadumez.com
https://www.pinterest.com/andydumez
https://www.instagram.com/andreea.dumez/

Made in the USA
Middletown, DE
20 October 2021